My Family

by Tammy Jones

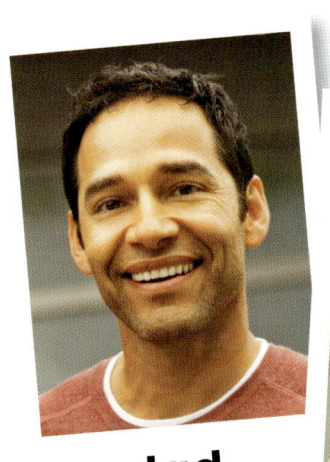

dad

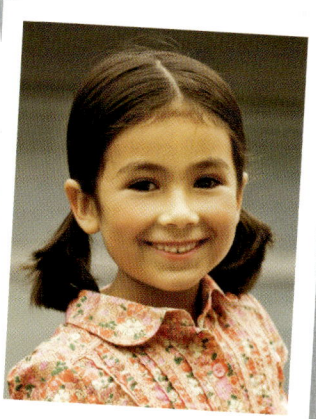

me

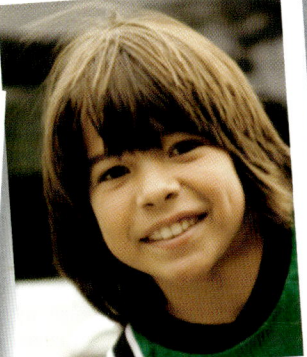

brother

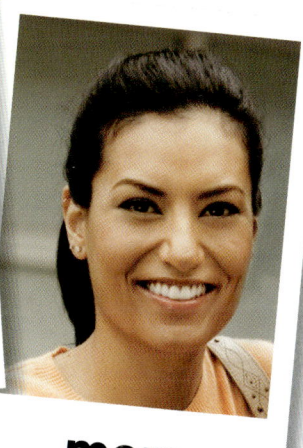

mom

Picture Words

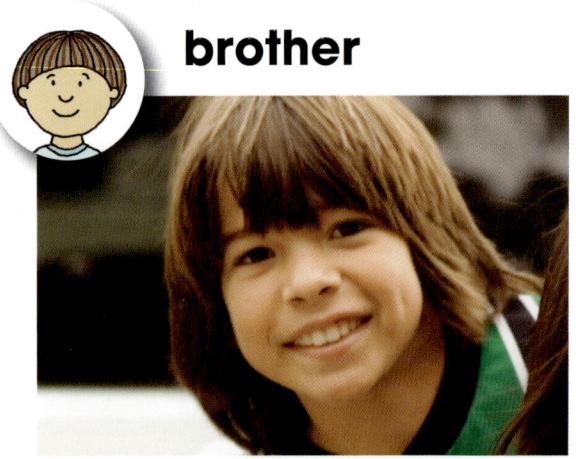

brother

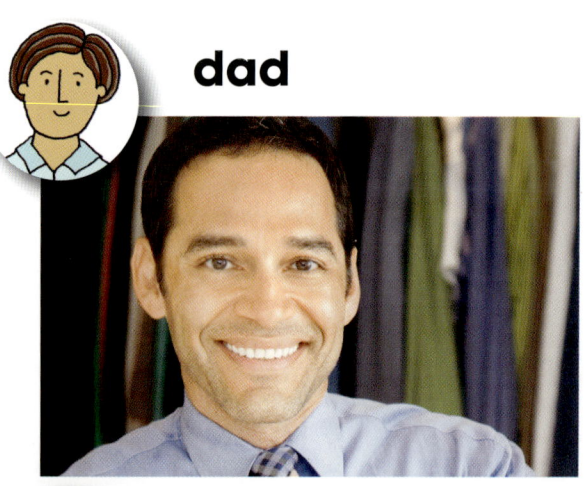

dad

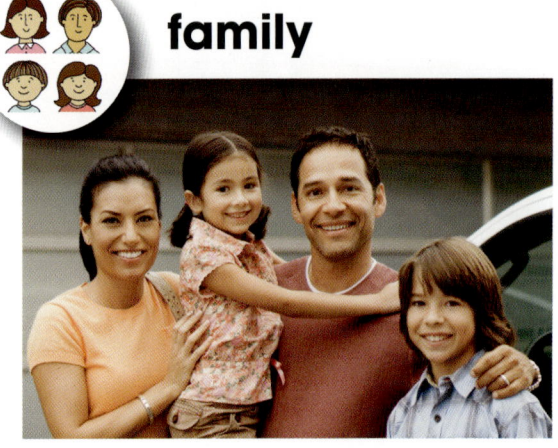

family

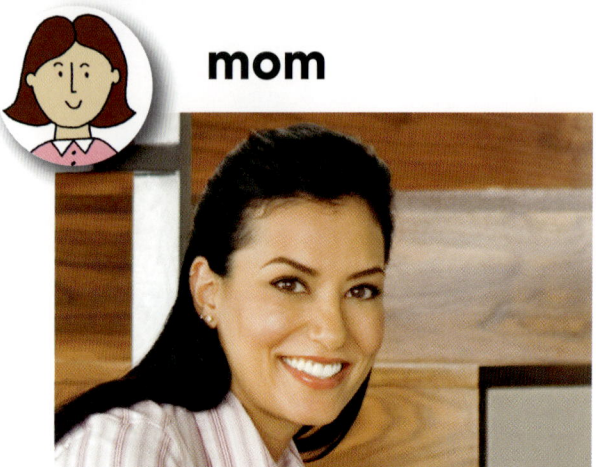

mom

Sight Words

is

me

my

this

This is my 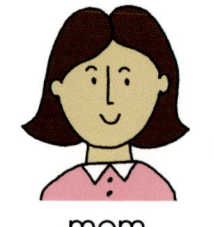 .

mom

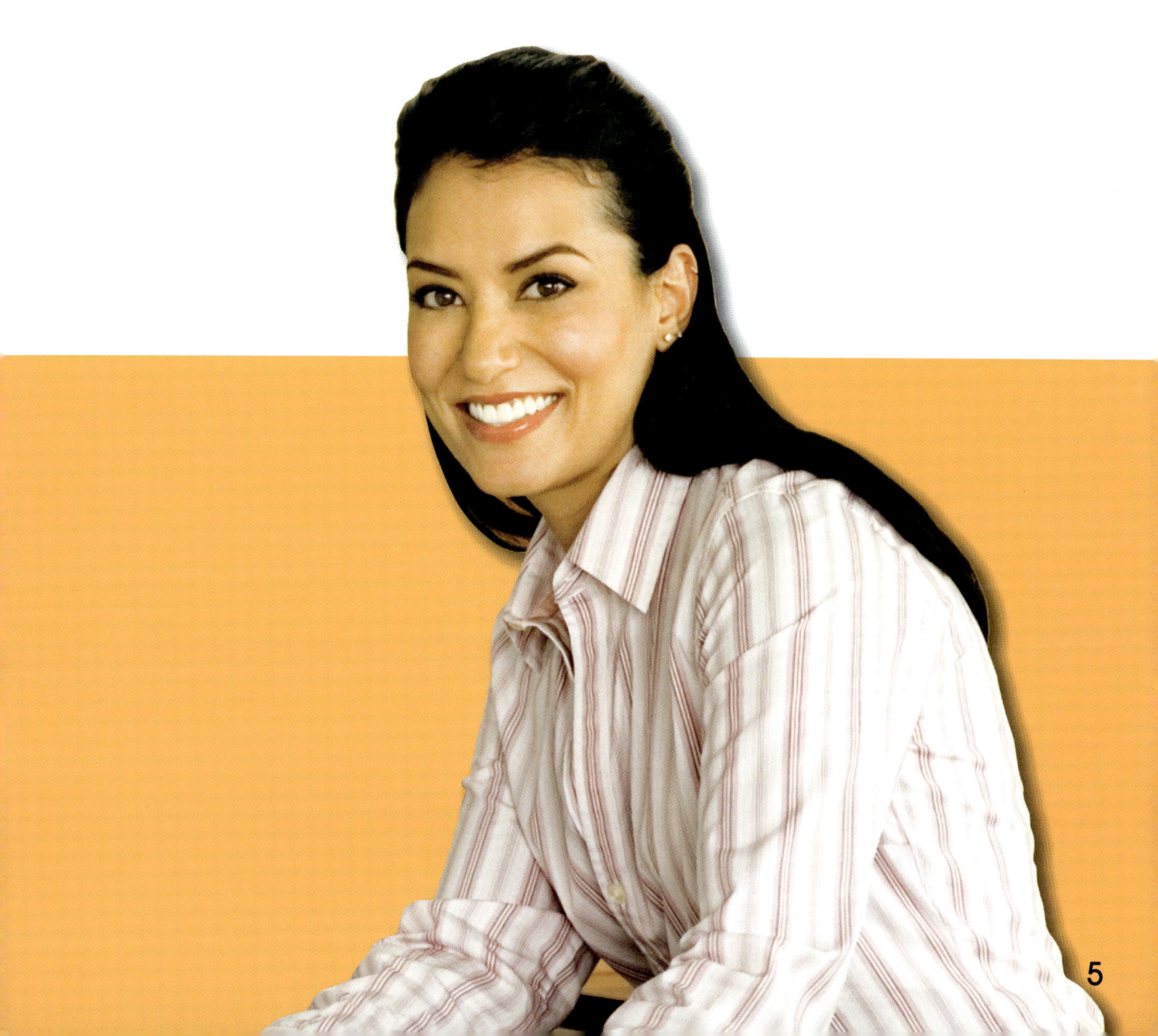

5

This is my .

dad

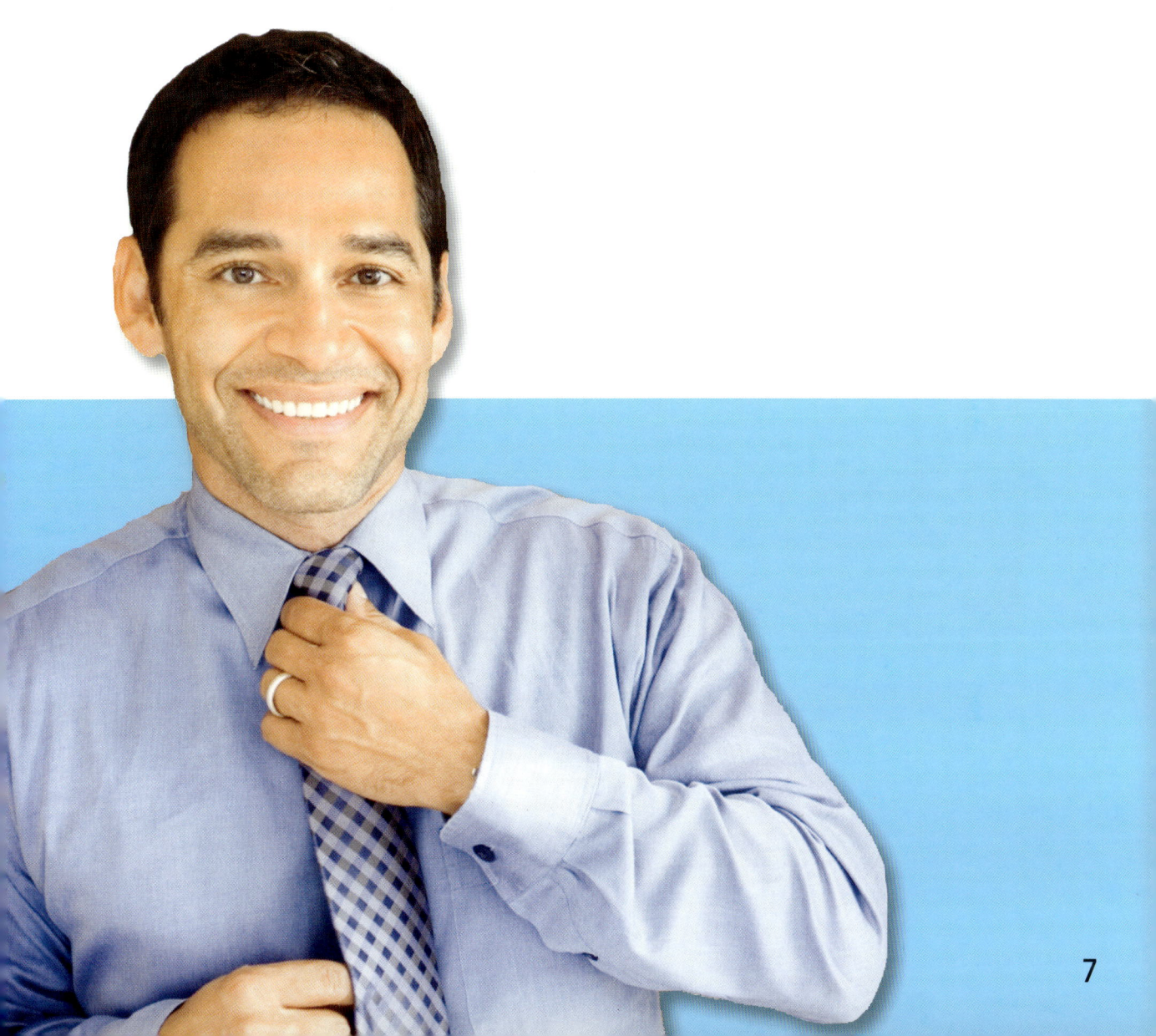

7

This is my .

brother

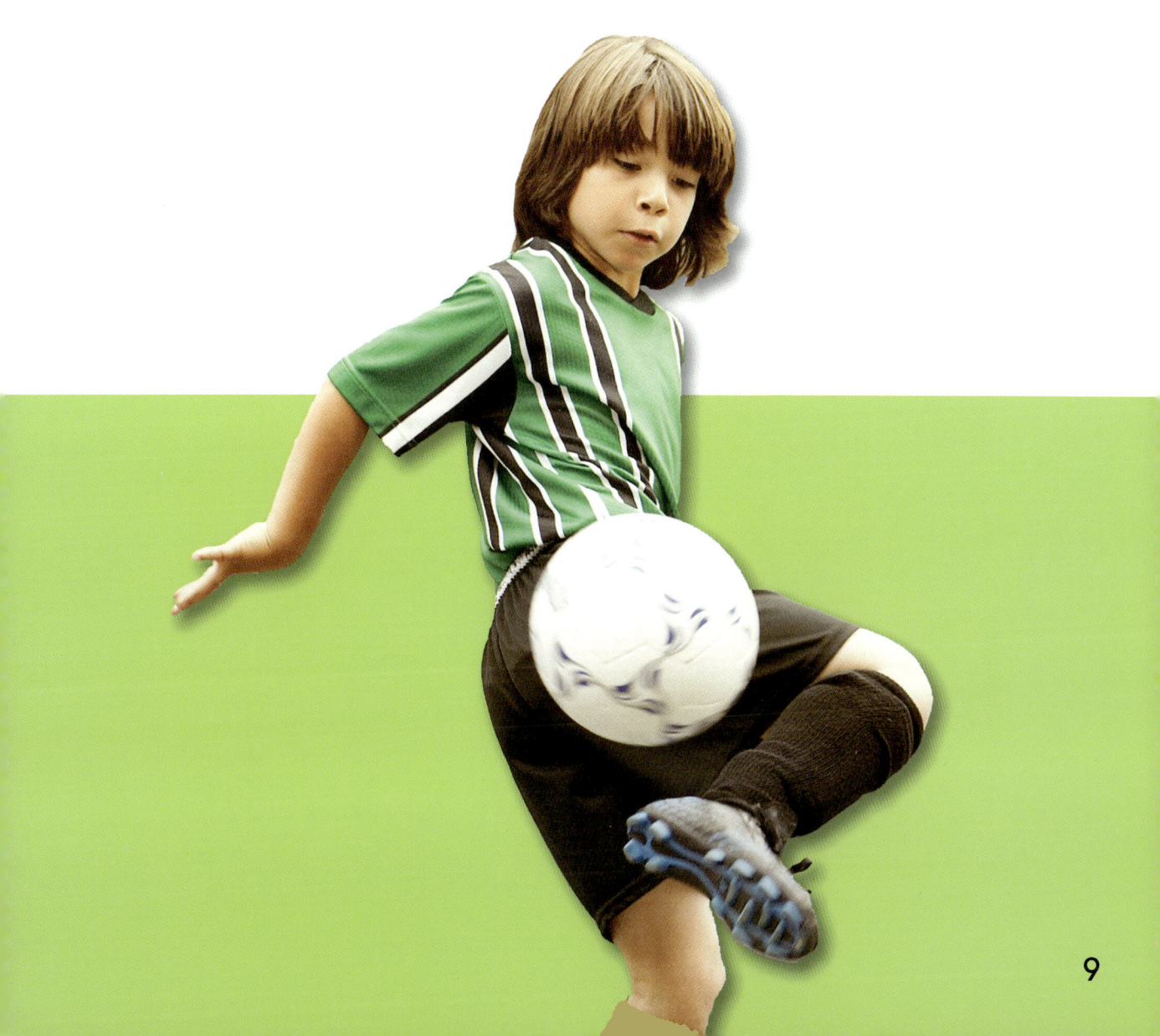

This is my .

family

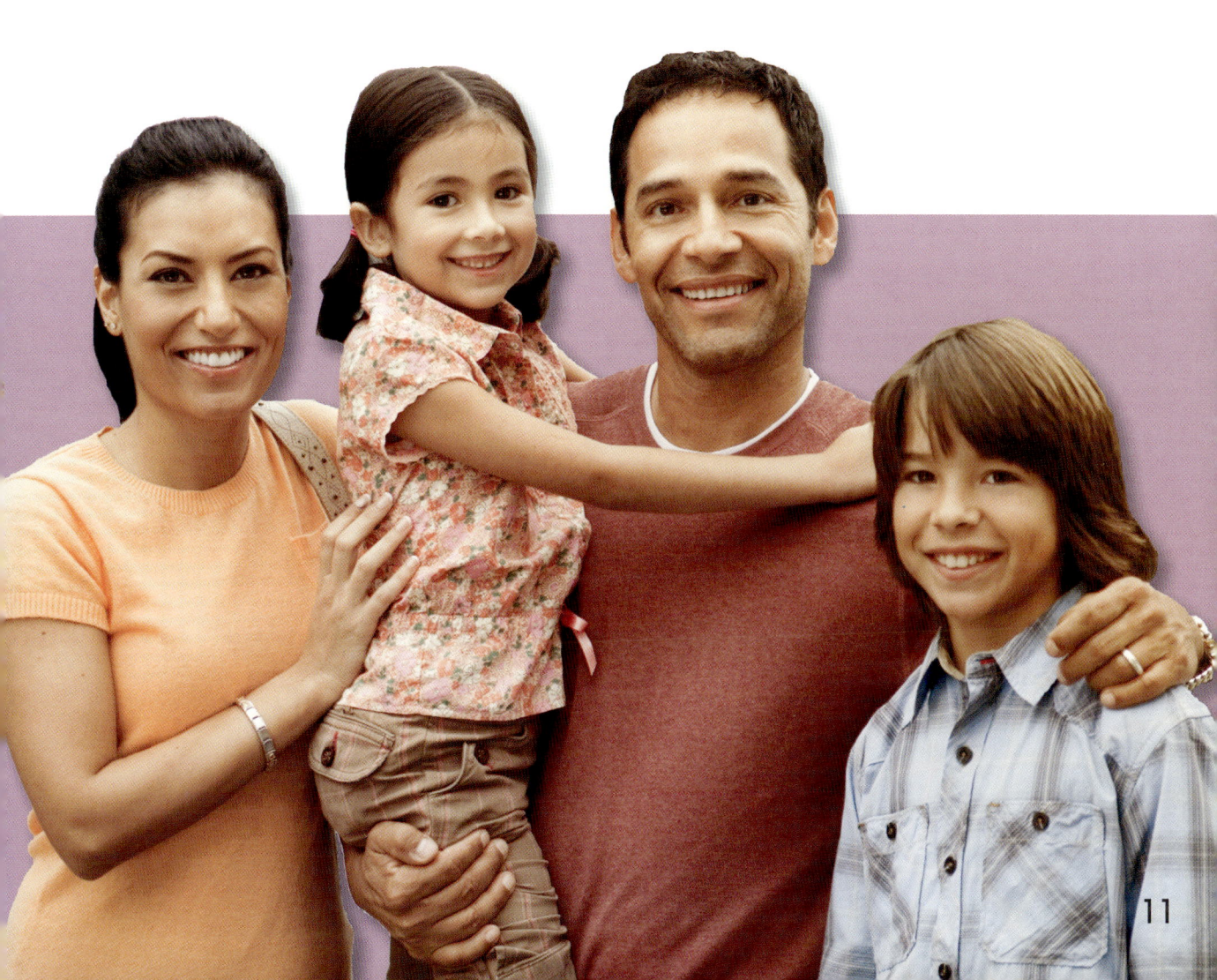

This is me.

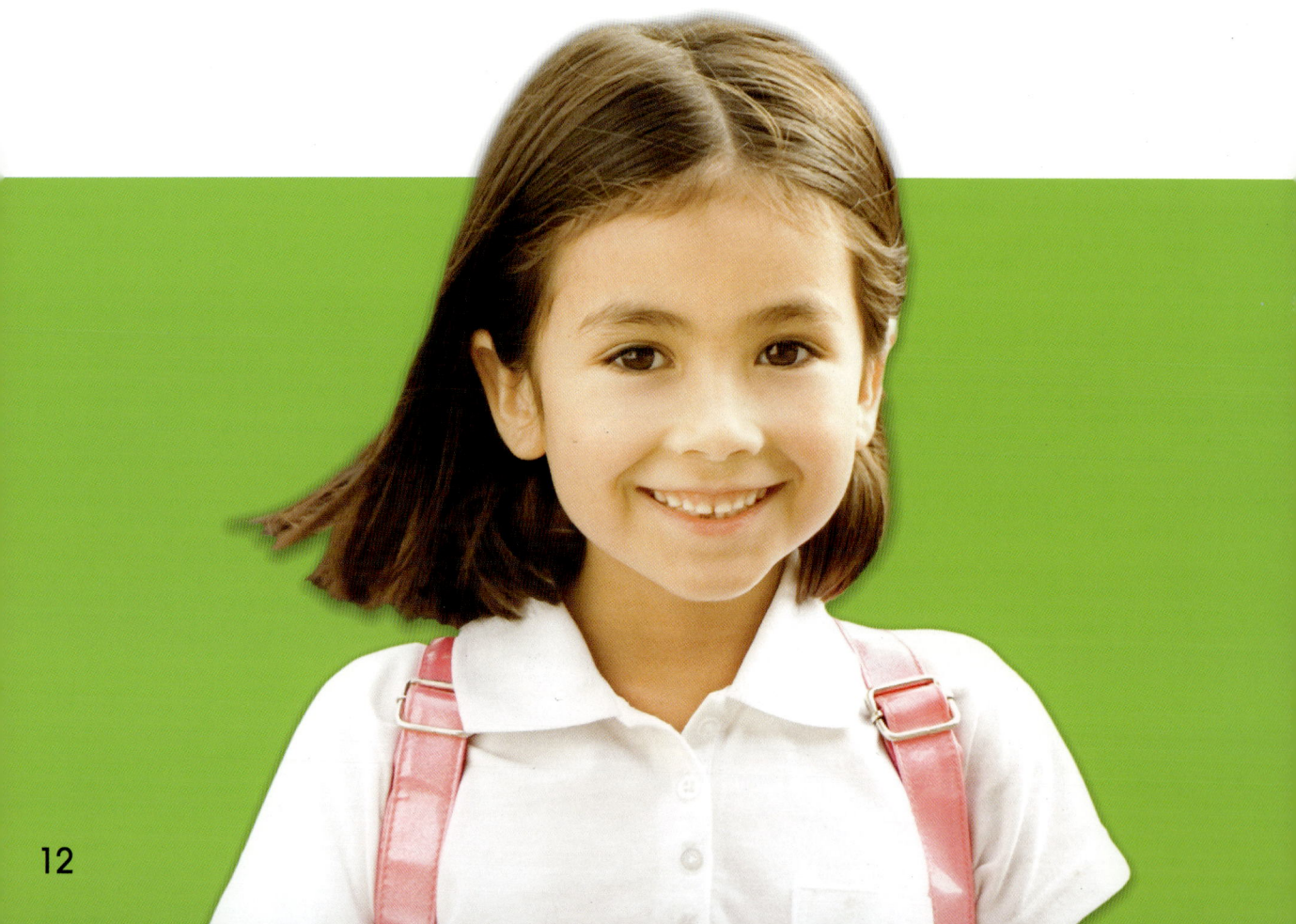